GOD'S CHISEL

BECOMING GOD'S MASTERPIECE

EDDIE **JAMES**
TOMMY **WOODARD**
THE SKIT GUYS

SkitGuys, Inc.

God's Chisel
Copyright © 2014 by Skit Guys, Inc.

Visit www.skitguys.com for more resources.

ISBN 978-0-9909464-0-3

Trade Paper Edition

If you come across an internet addresses (websites, blogs, etc.) or phone
number in here...they were correct when we first published this book. We're
not saying that they will always be there, so please be careful.

Cover design: Chris Castor
Interior design: David Conn

Printed in the United States of America

Dedicated to all the people that have asked God
to "chisel" their hearts and souls…
and lived to tell the tale.

Keep choosing the chisel.

We'd love to hear your chisel stories,
email us at chisel@skitguys.com.

CONTENTS

IS GOD'S MASTERPIECE

PREFACE

EDDIE

It was the year 2000.

That sounds so profound. ("*It was the year 2000.*")

We had just gotten through the world-coming-to-an-end scare, and I was newly married and on the verge of 30. What a combination.

Since I was 18, I had worked at a church in Southern California—Saddleback Valley Community Church. Home of Pastor Rick Warren and the Purpose Driven Life.

Coming from Oklahoma, this congregation opened me up to a God that I had never experienced.

Tom and I went out there one summer as interns. Tom went back to Oklahoma, and I ended up staying for a two-year internship that turned into eight great years.

I learned a ton about ministry. I also learned how to whip up a skit and perform it and have it ready for a weekend service. Whether it was for the student ministry or Rick calling on a Thursday wanting a skit that weekend, I learned very quickly how to assemble a team and put something together.

It was the equivalent of a comedian doing comedy clubs when I look back. There were six weekend services, so if I were doing a skit, we'd meet Saturday morning and put it together, and by 4 o'clock that afternoon we went live with our first performance. I had a great team—we'd go backstage after a performance and correct, rewrite, tweak, and get it ready to go again. By the end of a weekend, we had a great skit!

Hang on. I feel as though I should stop the car for a minute. I know "skit" has a negative connotation in the theatre world. It's viewed as something you do at a camp and an endeavor without merit. A "sketch" is what most folks call them, but to Tom and I, they've always been skits. We've tried to look at the cheesy-ness of church "sketches" and reimagine them as performances worth watching. We even call ourselves "The Skit Guys." I hold the name in high esteem: SKIT. These 10-minute slices of life can make one laugh and ponder. I love that.

Okay, back to the story.

I left California in 1996 and moved to Texas where Tom was married and working as a youth minister. Immediately we started getting calls to do our skits. I had a whole bag full of them coming from Saddleback. It was merely just a matter of grabbing them and turning many of them into a duo format rather than an ensemble.

So we spent the next four years creating "The Skit Guys." In 1999 I returned to Saddleback with my wife, and I was in charge of skits for the student ministry and had the honor and privilege of performing them on mainstage periodically for Rick and the worship services.

It was the year 2000. (See? I got us back around!) I was supposed to put together a skit to illustrate a Doug Fields talk—that we're all "original masterpiece" creations; the Scripture was Ephesians 2:10. I spent most of the week struggling to dream up a skit, but nothing came to mind. I was struggling in my own life, too. Since moving back my wife and I were broke and in debt. The money I was making doing skits and drama was just not paying off. It seemed like every gig that Tom and I were asked to do eventually got canceled. I had never experienced a season like that. It was dry. I felt called to come back and really hone my skills on how people could do drama at their own churches but first I had to learn and relearn. It wasn't easy.

I knew there was a Saturday night service, and I would need to provide at least "something." I had a fellow actress meet me at the church and told her I had nothing but hopefully something would pop before the service that night.

As I walked out of the garage to my car, I saw a hammer and chisel. I stood there looking at them for a minute. I thought, "That's how I feel right now—hammered upon. Like God has forgotten about me." I didn't feel like an "original masterpiece."

Then something clicked: *Isn't that how we become fully devoted followers of Christ? By going through the storms of life and becoming masterpieces?* I grabbed the hammer and chisel on my way to the church not knowing exactly what I was going to do, but I could see God using a hammer and chisel to gradually chip away the stuff that doesn't belong anymore. To correct and instruct us while taking away the things that takes away our faith. I envisioned God looking at his unfinished work—his child—with grace and truth. And if the believer is willing, she could "choose the chisel" and be molded in such a way that her life becomes a blessing for God and his Kingdom.

That weekend the "Chisel" skit was born. But it took almost a decade before people began connecting with it. And thanks to the help of a girl named "Cat Eyes" who started sharing "God's Chisel" online in 2009, it took on a life of its own. Even to this day, we're amazed at how far this video has gone all across the world.

As I look back—in that garage, staring at a hammer and

chisel—I remember the pain I was in. But the chiseling that was going on in my life is still happening today.

What I couldn't have imagined is what God wanted to do with this skit.

May you never grow weary as God chisels your own life.

Even during our most ordinary days, God is up to something.

Don't give up. God's not done with you—his original masterpiece.

Eddie James
(the Bald Skit Guy)

TOMMY

Fast-forward the tape a couple of years. Ed finishes wandering in the Southern California desert and comes home to Texas. He brings with him a wealth of wisdom (weird how suffering does that) and a treasure trove of skits.

As we continue to travel and perform, Ed would reach into his bag of skits and pull one out. (Mind you, he didn't really have a bag filled with skit scripts...that would be weird...kinda cool, but mostly weird.) He would say, "We did this skit at Saddleback—what do you think?" I would say, "Sounds good to me." (Which is what I say about most things.) Then we would figure out how to tweak it here and there and make it a Skit Guys' skit.

Then one day, it happened! Eddie reaches into his bag of skits, and one emerges that was glowing bright white. It's so bright I can't look at it! In the background the "Hallelujah" chorus is being sung. I turn around to what appears to be hundreds of angels singing at the top of their lungs. (Mind you, they were Muppet angels, but still very strong singers— all except Gonzo, who was playing the trumpet.) Then Jim Caviezel appears to me and says, "Go ahead, do the skit." He's speaking Aramaic but fortunately there are subtitles in my vision. I knew this was going to be powerful.

Okay, so it wasn't exactly like that. It was more like—we needed a serious skit at an event we were doing and Ed said,

"We did this skit at Saddleback. It's about God chiseling things out of a woman's life. We could change it to a man and do that skit."

I said, "Sounds good. How does it end?"

He said, "She pulls a snowflake out of her back pocket, and God tells her how she is unique like a snowflake."

I said, "Sounds like we need a new ending, 'cause I'm not pulling a snowflake out of my back pocket."

So we came up with a new ending and started performing what we called "The Chisel Skit." It was so powerful, so pro- found...and so painful! Seriously, there were times I would come home from an event and my wife Angie would ask, "What happened to your back?" I would say, "We did the chisel skit." She would reply, "It looks like it hurt." She had no idea.

It hurt every time and still does. Not the times Ed would impale me with a misfired chisel. That wasn't a big deal. It was (and still is) the conversations I have with God onstage. You see, while I consider myself a bit of an actor, it takes no acting skills for me to perform this skit. Each time we perform it, I get to have a conversation with God in front of an audience. While I know the storyline and 90 percent of what I'll say and what he'll say, it still gets me every time.

Thing is, I know who I am when no one is looking. I know

what's in my life that needs to be chiseled out. But I've never gotten used to hearing God say, "I love you too much to leave you where you are" or "Don't compare yourself to anyone else—that's trivial nonsense" or "You are my original masterpiece."

These statements connect with my soul—a soul that longs to be different. They pierce my heart and remind me that I have a purpose upon this crazy world. And no matter what my condition…God loves me.

In some form or fashion, God is chiseling me every time we perform the skit. While it hurts, I love it. Because at the end of the day, my greatest desire is to simply be who God created me to be. If that's your desire—or even if you just can't seem to make sense of the seemingly random things God brings into or allows into your life—then this book is for you.

So please join me and my best friend Ed as we walk through the chiseling process. But consider yourself warned: It's gonna hurt, and it may leave some marks. But hey, at least you won't have to throw away a shirt because it has little holes with your bloodstains on it. (It only happened once, and I didn't tell Ed, so let's keep that between us.)

Tommy Woodard
(the Skit Guy with hair and back scars)

Our hope and prayer is that this book, along with the video, can minister to your heart like it has ours.

"Heavenly Father, thank you for accepting us as we are, but loving us too much to leave us this way. We pray for the reader of this book: Help them to deal with the stuff you want chiseled out of their life. Prepare their hearts for this wonderful process of becoming the people you planned for us to be. While it may be tough at times, your grace is sufficient all the time. May this be a great journey of freedom in you."

IN THE BEGINNING...

We know that line has already been used at the beginning of another book. Don't judge—in fact, everything in this book is based on that book...the Bible

Actually everyone's life story has a beginning. However, that beginning is not birth. Your life story and my life story began way before we were born.

Our story began with God's thought of us.

Not unlike a sculptor who begins chipping away at her unformed objects.

You see, before one piece of marble, limestone, or granite falls to the floor, the sculptor has a thought. An image is formed in her mind, and it becomes living things—it comes to life there.

The sculptor can see what he wants the shape to become:

the sleek mane of a horse that flows this way and that in the wind. (Like those wild horses in all those westerns.) The tense muscles of a warrior armed and ready for battle. (You know, like *Braveheart* with a "gentler" Mel Gibson.) The soft lines of two lovers embracing each other. (What!? You just mentioned lovers in a Christian publication! Relax. We're implying that the lovers in the sculpture are married.) Whatever the image in the mind of the sculptor, he sees it in detail. He allows it to breathe and live—and in so doing captures the essence of what is going to be created.

DO YOU REALIZE THAT YOU WEREN'T HASTILY THROWN TOGETHER AT THE LAST MINUTE BY THE CREATOR?

Have you ever hastily started a project? If you attended middle school, you have. You know, the night before or even the morning a class project is due, you remember it. The idea pops into your mind, and you rush into it, only to realize that you weren't prepared for steps 2, 3, or 4. And suddenly you're in knee deep. You can't make heads or tails of what you initially wanted to do, and you have to abandon it. Because an "F" on a project is easier to stomach than standing in front of your friends and peers trying to explain that the Styrofoam cups attached to an old "Happy Birthday" plate represents the possibility of extraterrestrial life. Anyway you slice it, it's just a total loss.

Well, when you're attempting to chisel stone, imagine the consequence of rushing. You can't just glue an arm back on. If you forget a piece, it's gone. If you didn't take the time to get the hair just right, you'll end up with Donald Trump when you were going for Justin Bieber. There aren't second chances in the world of sculpture. When you start down a path, you are committed. (By the way, why were you carving a statue of Justin Bieber in the first place?)

Do you realize that you weren't hastily thrown together at the last minute by the Creator? God thought about you and he THINKS about you. Yes, you—with everything in your past, all your baggage, and that long list of hang-ups, temper tantrums,"unlovable" qualities—even the way you eat Cheetos and wipe your cheesy fingers on the couch. God thinks about you!

Just like a sculptor imagining the work that's about to be done, God takes great delight in thinking about you. And just as the sculptor thinks about the work of art he's making and continues thinking about it until he's finished, God never stops thinking about us.

Because God is never finished with us. We are a constant work-in-progress. As soon as God chisels something out of our lives or builds up something great in us, there will always be something else to work on or build. That's the work of God's chisel.

BECAUSE GOD IS NEVER FINISHED WITH US. WE ARE A CONSTANT WORK-IN-PROGRESS.

Thing is, what tends to happen in this dance with God is that we—his creations—don't want to submit to the work. It's as if we've said, "This is as good as I get."

But there is more to you than that. Isn't it time we give more thought to how God made us and what he wants to do in us and through us?

Yes. It's time to choose the chisel.

SELECTING THE STONE

After the idea takes shape in the mind of the artist, they seek out the stone. The artist has been living with this idea in their mind; they know what it's going to take to bring this piece to life. They don't want to choose a stone that's too big...or small. Like Goldilocks, they are looking for one that is "just right." The artist knows where the sculpture is going to live, what light it will be under, what conditions it will need to withstand, all these things will go into the selection of the stone.

The Bible refers to us as clay pottery and God is the potter. We are clay—water and dirt. Sure, we're formed in the master's hands...but still water and dirt. (BTW: This is a great argument against your mom when she is mad that you got dirty. "Really mom? I'm in trouble for getting more of me on me!?") God has an idea with you in mind. Your life, your dreams, your visions – the plans can come to fruition in different ways when we live a life to make him famous instead of ourselves. Many times, we take the reins away from God and say, "you aren't doing it fast enough." Or, "I got this God. I may not like your outcome so let me work this a little bit and I'll hand it back over." We do the selecting; we do the fast-forwarding of our lives and say to God and everyone else, "this is what's best for me." We've truly left God out of the equation. Think about it...think about all the times you've controlled a situation. You may have said you have surrendered to the Lord but not fully trusted him.

God has chosen you. The stone, the clay, the dirt. He has an idea in mind. Will you let him mold you into the image in his mind?

THE TOOLS

The tools of the sculptor are basic. First, a striking instrument...a mallet or hammer. This is used to strike the chisel. There are a variety of hammers that the sculptor can choose. Do they need a heavy blow to remove big chunks of stone or do they need a lighter touch to evoke a smile from the piece.

GOD'S CHISEL

The artist knows what the piece of art needs and chooses the right tool for the task at hand. (For the record, our preferred hammer is still the MC Hammer. Can't touch this!)

Next, the chisels. Yep, that's right...plural. There are numerous chisels that a sculptor can choose from, each with a different tip and purpose. There's a blunt chisel; this is typically used in the early stages, to remove large chunks of stone and get the basic form to reveal itself from the stone. And then there are others that will shape the stone in different ways; from smooth surfaces to delicate lines in the stone, each chisel is chosen for the task at hand. Whatever the sculptor is trying to pull from the stone, they will grab that tool and use it upon the stone. The image that the artist has seen tells it which chisel will work best.

Finally, the artist will use some sort of abrasive upon the stone. Whether sandpaper or some sort of pumice, the sculptor will work on the piece to get each line just right. The smooth skin isn't achieved with the blow of a hammer and chisel. Rather, the artist will lovingly and painstakingly work the "skin" of the piece. Each crease and crevice will be rubbed by the artist's hand. Each part caressed by the pumice to get just the right look and feel. Without this loving embrace, the piece would have a rough quality to it. Which is not good unless you are making a sculpture of your mother-in-law! (Note to the publisher: Please strike this line from the books we give to our in-laws!)

We've all seen an unfinished piece of art, right? You know what that looks like...sometimes they look better than others, but you always know that wasn't how the artist saw it in their mind. For some reason though, the piece was left unfinished. An unfinished piece of art leaves the viewer unsettled. We look and wonder "Why?" What happened? It was not for a lack of idea or ability. But somewhere along the way, something happened to disrupt the process of the artist.

THE PROCESS

And now the process. With the image in mind, the stone chosen and the tools gathered, the artist is ready to create. And again, there's a specific process that the sculptor uses. It's not by happenstance that the stone will undergo a transformation from a piece that has no form to a living piece of art. There are three main steps that a sculpture will go through: roughing out, refining, and finishing.

Just so this feels more like a book for those of you who need to see the "big picture"—here's what these three steps look like "CliffsNotes" version. BTW—If it wasn't for Cliff giving us his notes, we wouldn't have had all that time to go to the movies and play video games...Thank you Cliff!

Roughing Out

As soon as the sculptor is ready he or she will begin the process by roughing out the stone. This is typically done with a heavy mallet and a chisel that is equally heavy and possesses a broad head. The goal at this stage is to remove the "large chunks" of stone that ensnare the piece. Great care is taken to not remove too much stone, because you can't get it back. Like loaning money to your teenage child...you'll never get that back, either! They'll utilize the mallet and chisel and get rid of any unwanted pieces of stone.

Refining

At this point, the sculptor won't strike the chisel with the same force as before. They'll use a variety of chisels to pull the general shape of the piece from the stone. You'll begin to see texture added at this point in the process and the whole piece begins to take a more recognizable form. No longer is the piece a large chunk of stone; at this point the piece begins to take shape.

Finishing

The sculptor begins to use fine tools to finish the piece. Whether a rasp, or a piece of pumice or sandpaper, the piece succumbs to the artist's desires and finally reaches completion. This is the most intimate part of the process. The artist is taking the time to smooth over the rough areas that were worked on earlier. Only the artist knows when the piece is complete. Why? Because it was his idea from the very beginning. The piece of art does not decide what it will be, the sculptor does.

So now that we got our feet wet and waded in the shallow end of this book you have picked up...are you ready to choose the chisel? Are you ready to explore what God has in store for you? Before you answer that—keep it here and answer these questions on the next page. I know—it's work. Right now you are saying, "Where am I going to find a pencil?!" or "I don't want to have to think! This is mere toilet reading." Great things come to those who do the work of the soul. Gandhi said that...or was it Benjamin Franklin? Wait...we just Googled it and apparently we made it up!

CHISEL Q'S:

1. Make a list of the top five "stressors" in your life. Imagine them as stones.

   1. _Financial_
   2. _Forgiveness and anger_
   3. _Criticism all the time._ _What I don't do right_
   4. _Family stress me out._
   5.

   • Which one is the biggest?
   Finance that I have money to pay

   • Which one is like a pebble that you can't get out of your shoe? _My Financial were I'm peace at._

   • Which one is going to be impossible to move without help? _Forgiveness and Anger_

2. Imagine your "Toolbox for Life."
   • Do you have an old wooden box with dozens of well-worn tools piled randomly or do you have one of those space-age tool cabinets with the polished tools laid perfectly inside the self-closing drawers?
   old Box with dozen of worn tools

   • Which do you wish you had? Which do you actually have? _I have a very used tool Box piled random._

- Who do you know in your own life that has one kind of toolbox or the other? *D I*

- What do you think God's toolbox looks like?
  Uses every tool in his toolbox

- If God is the sculptor and you are the stone, write down one thing you think God sees in you that no one else sees? *I see that I am stronger than I think*

- When you pull off a bandage do you yank it or peel it slowly? *Peel slowly*

- Sometimes we resist the sculptor because we know it's going to hurt. Don't say their name aloud but think of someone who is buried in stone, but can't let go of their rubble because they're afraid of the artist's chisel. Write down their initials and say a prayer for them.

- What are you hanging on to that you don't need? *My Anger, not Forgiving*

3. The introduction talks about "The Process" (Roughing Out, Refining, Finishing). This can mean your own life as a whole or individual problems you face each day. Think of some problem or some hard time you've been through in your life. Can you see the whole process looking back on it?

- When facing a problem which area do you tend to spend the most time? *How to make it work 3 how.*

- Do you think "the process" is life as a whole or something that happens over and over?

- Which process is the most difficult?

4. Write down a part of your life you feel is "finished." Something that took a long time to go through but now is a work of art to you. *It's not finished yet.*

PRAY THIS PRAYER:

God sometimes I feel like an action figure inside an ice cube in the freezer. How can I break free if I can't even move? Help me, God. Open my mind and my heart to the possibilities in these pages. Help me learn. Help me see your guiding hand in creating me into the person you have called me to be. Amen.

CHISEL STORY

I have asked God to chisel away all my anger, the empty feeling I have in my heart all the time, and feeling worthless and unworthy of God and his love. I'm still trying to give God full control of my entire life, but knowing that it is what he wants for me and that I am not worthless or junk, it makes it easier.

Drew

Okay...now turn the page. Quit stalling — it's time to choose the chisel.

CHAPTER 1
YOUR STORY & GOD'S PLACE IN IT

CHISEL QUOTE:

Ephesians 2:10 says that we "are God's workmanship created in Christ Jesus to do good works." That word "workmanship" comes from the Greek word "poiEma." We get the word "poem" from that same word. So in a sense, we are God's poem...or his masterpiece. Now I don't know about you, but when I get up in the morning and look in the mirror, I don't see a masterpiece. (I mean, maybe a Picasso.) But I want to be everything God intends for me to be. So I go to him and pray, "Dear Heavenly Father, make me everything you want me to be. Mold me into the image of your Son."

SCRIPTURE

Your hands made me and formed me. Give me understanding so that I might learn your commands. — Psalms 119:73

Yet, LORD, you are our father. We are the clay, and you are our potter; we are all the product of your labor. — Isaiah 64:8

Once upon a time...

Many stories begin with "once upon a time." And depending on the story, the action may come quickly...or it may take a little while to build...but the action will come.

Something happens. Somebody hurts someone else, and invariably the characters in our story are changed. These changes and plot twists encourage us to continue reading the book.

It's the same in our lives. We all have a once-upon-a-time beginning, too. Some of us grew up with two parents and our "once upon a time" began when those two people met, fell in love, and decided to bring new life into the world.

**GOD LONGS TO CALL OUT THE LOVE
THAT BROUGHT US INTO THE WORLD AND,
THROUGH US, UNLEASH IT UPON THE WORLD.**

Others have different stories that may involve heartache at the beginning…but there was always love. At the core of each of our stories is a flicker, a glimmer of love…it may have been small, but it was always present.

Of course our stories contain different twists and turns, heroes and monsters, but at the end of the day, each of our stories is **our story**. It's unique. No one else can lay claim to the life that each of us have lived. No one else made the choices we made…or will make in the future.

Our story is our story, but…and this is a big "but," none of our stories are complete. Not yet. There's a character or a plot twist in our story that we may not have encountered, but it's about to alter our story. And like an author that is writing a better story, God is calling us into something different. God knows the shape of our lives…God knows who we really are and who we can truly become.

Think about that for a minute. What would you like to become? If you could do anything with your life, knowing you wouldn't fail, what would you do? The sad part is even with a question like this, most of us make excuses as to why these things will never come to pass. Our race has started, but our hearts aren't in the race because of guilt over our past dalliances, addictions, and wrong choices.

But God is longing for a story change in our lives. God

longs to call out the love that brought us into the world and, through us, unleash it upon the world. The process of roughing out then, in each of our lives, is the process God uses to reveal more of Jesus. At our core, in our innermost being, we've been marked by God and marked for love.

Keeping the idea of the author/creator in mind, let's change gears a little and look at it in the light of a sculptor and his work. As we noted, a sculptor starts with an image in his mind. He sees what the lump of stone will become, and so it is with the Ultimate Sculptor. God sees what others only get glimpses of...and instead of seeing us as we are, God sees us as who we can become.

KNIT TOGETHER

Think about what David wrote in Psalm 139.

As you read this Psalm, make it personal. Notice what King David (with all his character flaws) observes regarding how God viewed him. Take notes beside the verses about things that come to your heart and mind regarding how God loves you. (Yes, more work! AAAGHH!!) This is part of the "roughing out" process.

Certainly you made my mind and heart;
You wove me together in my mother's womb.
I will give you thanks because your deeds are awesome
 and amazing.

You knew me thoroughly;

my bones were not hidden from you,

when I was made in secret

and sewed together in the depths of the earth.

Your eyes saw me when I was inside the womb.

All the days ordained for me

were recorded in your scroll

before one of them came into existence.

How difficult it is for me to fathom your thoughts about
me, O God!

How vast is their sum total!

If I tried to count them,

they would outnumber the grains of sand.

GOD DOESN'T MAKE JUNK! SO, NO MATTER WHAT OTHER PEOPLE HAVE SAID, NO MATTER WHAT THAT TINY LITTLE VOICE IN YOUR HEAD SAYS— THEY ARE LIARS.

So, you've read it. You even did some ninja moves as far as soul searching goes, and you're beginning to look in the mirror and maybe realizing for the first time: GOD DOESN'T MAKE JUNK! So, no matter what other people have said, no matter what that tiny little voice in your head says—they are liars. What does Psalm 139 say about the number of times God thinks about you? That they outnumber the grains of sand. Think about a beach or a desert. The sand goes on and on and on. The Creator of the Universe thinks of you more than those grains of sand. Isn't that amazing?

Now that you've had time to read and process this, write down what your "old life" looks like and what you want your "new life" to look like.

We get that the "old life" may be some ways of living that are still continuing. Some destructive habits, some possessive relationships, a bad habit that has you imprisoned. BUT (we love saying "but") this is your *old* life. The life you want to give up so you can get to something else. This is the ROUGH stuff.

So let's talk about it. Write down the stuff that doesn't work in your world anymore. Just a little encouragement: If you do the work in this book, this will become a cherished book.

Then move on to the promising page—your NEW life. Your new world. Write down—even if there's some fear involved— what you'd like to see happen in this new world. This new chapter of your "once upon a time." That's the great part about the stories we read. The stories change. The characters grow up, and so we must grow up as well. (Okay put down the bottle and take off the diaper—tough love time—start writing!)

OLD LIFE:

You were taught with reference to your former way of life to lay aside the old man who is being corrupted in accordance with deceitful desires, to be renewed in the spirit of your mind, and to put on the new man who has been created in God's image—in righteousness and holiness that comes from truth.—Ephesians 4:22-24

He must become more important while I become less important.—(John 3:30)

NEW LIFE:

So then, if anyone is in Christ, he is a new creation; what is old has passed away—look, what is new has come! —2 Corinthians 5:17

At our best and at our worst, God knows us. And just like it was for David, it's too difficult for us to even comprehend. The God of the universe knew you as you were being created. Knit together.

Let's look at David:

WORST:	BEST:
Liar	Brave
Adulterer	Faithful
Murderer	Obedient
Selfish	Humble
Irresponsible	Kind
Jealous	Patient
Lustful	Loving
Egotistical	Worshipful

If God can take someone like David and still call him a man after his own heart, doesn't it stand to reason that we can stay in the race and finish out the story God has for us? Think about it: On your worst day...God loves you. On your best day...God loves you. No performance necessary when it comes to the Creator of the Universe.

You are good. God created you in his image. His good image. That is what makes you good. Your "goodness" is not a statement in regard to your actions or thoughts—you know they're not always good. Rather you being good is a statement about the Author and Creator of life who made you good. In the beginning God saw that his creation was good. (Genesis 1:31) We may make the excuse, "I can't be good," but God replies, "I made you Good."

Be honest: If you were to have a toe-to-toe, knee-to-knee talk with God, and he makes that statement to you...are you really going to come back with a, "Yeah, but..."?

Speaking of "buts" have you thought about how many "Yeah, but" excuses you make, day in and day out? It's time to get off our "buts." (See the pun? Oh, how we love it!) It's time to start roughing out these walls in our lives and knocking them down and realizing the Creator made us and knit us together in the womb.

I had the honor of being a part of the first Celebrate Recovery in Mission Viejo, California. The founder, John Baker was my sponsor in those early days. He said a lot to me in those days, but one of the phrases that kept coming up was: "Eddie, be gentle on yourself."

You see, I was what you would call a "people pleaser." I didn't like myself...to the point that I craved other people's approval. It was great for an actor—I could hide behind different characters, being the "funny guy" but never really having to grow up and deal with my own pain and regret. To top it off, I worked at a church—I got to help people instead of dealing with my baggage. Those two things combined let me put off the work I needed to do on myself. It was a horrible combination. I would beat myself up for anything and everything. If I did something good – I'd pick it apart and find something I could have done better. If I did something not so great, I'd nitpick it in my brain to the point of compulsion – all the while waiting for my next "fix" of making someone smile or like me or feeling like I did a good job. Talk about insanity. I put the fun in "dysfunction." It took me some time to be gentle on the person God was chiseling and to realize I was worth fighting for…in essence that I was good enough.

AND AS OUR STONE STARTS TO FEEL GOD'S CHISEL, AND THE CHUNKS AND CHIPS OF OUR LIVES FALL AROUND OUR FEET, AND THE REGRETS IN OUR HEARTS START TO DISAPPEAR, YOU NEED TO REMEMBER THAT GOD SEES THE REAL YOU.

There is a reason for each of our stories. We will say it again: **You are good.**

From this passage, we get another great glimpse at our Sculptor. God isn't a sculptor who's stepping into the scene late in our stories…rather, God sees beneath all the hard, calcified rock that has built up around the "real" you. God sees what he created. And as the writer of Genesis said:

God created humankind in his own image,
in the image of God he created them,
male and female he created them...
God saw all that he had made—and it was very good!

The image that God sees when he looks at you...when God looks at your neighbor...is a good image. And as our stone starts to feel God's chisel, and the chunks and chips of our lives fall around our feet, and the regrets in our hearts start to disappear, you need to remember that God sees the real you. As he works on our hearts, as he works on our minds, as he works on our eyes, mouths...as God works on our beings, great care is being taken to reveal the creation that he saw at the very beginning of our story.

Sure, a lot of stuff has grown up around our hearts, stuff that's trying to strangle any image of God that might make an appearance. But with careful precision, God removes the largest pieces of stone and rock that have warped the image he saw in the beginning.

Do you see what God sees? Maybe this chapter has made you smile. You've seen you aren't junk, and your story can have an ending where you get to make God famous with your life. Or maybe this chapter has been a little "rough." As you take a hard look at the "rough" edges of your life, you've seen much sin, many mistakes, and even a hint of a feeling that "there's no way God can see me as David describes in Psalm 139. At best, God is tolerating me!"

Friend, God loves you. Cares for you. Thinks about you. If you live near a beach, go now! When you get there, check out the vastness of his love. If you don't…well…Google "How many grains of sand can you fit in a coffee cup?" (We did it and it's over 1,000,000…That's a lot of thoughts and that's just one cup.) Sit there with the neon bulbs of the computer showing you but a sliver of what God's love looks like. Probably one of the best things you could do in front of a computer actually…

Okay, you made it through chapter 1—almost. Here are some questions for you to answer:

CHISEL Q'S

1. Let's cast a movie, okay? You're the casting director and the movie is called *David*. Thinking about everything you know about David...who would you cast in the lead role?

2. Right now, pull out your cell phone. Go ahead, even if you're in church, we give you permission. (Your teachers can write to US and complain.) Got your phone? Okay. Now take the number of your birth month. Count down that number from the top of your "people" list. Send a text to that person and say, "YOU ARE NOT JUNK."

3. Okay, it would be real easy to skip that last one wouldn't it? If you are reading this one and didn't send a text go back and do it now.

4. Quick Quiz. What word does God NEVER say? Not once. Not ever. What word has God never ever, ever, ever, ever said? Ready? The word is "Oops." Think like one of the great theologians and ponder that statement. God has never said "Oops." This means you...yes you...right now are a unique and wonderful and amazing creation of the Creator. We can't even see you from here and we still KNOW it's true.

5. Read Psalm 139. Read it twice. Now choose one line that somehow speaks to you and rewrite that line inserting your own name. No, not like "Your thoughts are TOMMY to me, oh God." (That's funny, but you know what we mean.) Write that "speaks-to-you line" with your name inserted. Now, if you are not already in trouble, text it to yourself. Why did you pick that particular line? What about the rest of the Psalm; what kind of day was David having?

6. The Psalmist here is writing about how absolutely huge God is. Think about the utter BIG-ness of God. God who made the microbes in drops of water you see in the microscope…God who made the planets that revolve around the sun that we can only see as a star in the night sky and know there are millions more beyond that. The God who made mountains and gave eagles wings and carved out the waterfalls and absolutely had a hand in the creation of both Reese's Peanut Butter Cups and coffee…

   Think about THAT God. Now, try to understand that David wants you to know that YOU are God's favorite creation. How does that make you feel?

Imagine you are going to the airport. You have six or eight bags with you. Everything you need: laptop, book bag, lunch bag, suitcase, garment bag, second suitcase, and on and on. You're struggling your way through the airport trying to get to the ticket counter. Are you your bags? Is the luggage you? No, it's what you carry with you. It is NOT you. When we say you are God's favorite creation, God sees the YOU beneath the bags, the same way God sees the YOU under the stone.

CHISEL STORY

The first time I saw God's Chisel I was afraid. The thought of giving up all control of my life seemed like something that was too hard to do. To be his meant to fully surrender my life. To die to self and to live in Christ. I am just a simple 21-year-old college student from the Philippines and God was desiring so much from me, but I also realized God has already given so much to me. He gave it all for me.

Michael

I was chiseled...very slowly and carefully by The Master Chiseler. He became and was The Only One I trusted to painfully remove my heart that demanded control; who wanted to do things myself; and who constantly was reliving past mistakes; and unable to forgive my own self for them.

Linda

PRAYER:

God, I am ready to soar. I want to run and throw my arms out and soar but I can't even move. I'm ready to get rid of the baggage God. I'm ready for you to use the chisel. There is something amazing underneath all this rock but I can't get rid of it on my own. I am ready God. Let's go to work. Amen.

CHAPTER 2
REFINING: DEALING WITH OUR OWN STUFF

CHISEL QUOTE

God: You know what insanity is? Insanity is doing the same thing over and over again and expecting different results. You've been doing some destructive things since you were a kid and it's insane. Allow me to chisel these out of your life. Allow me to produce character where you keep focusing so much on your image.

You: Yeah, but I was thinking...

God: Your thoughts are not my thoughts.

You: Well, I was figuring if we could go another way...

God: Your ways are not my ways.

SCRIPTURE

Indeed, my plans are not like your plans,
and my deeds are not like your deeds,
for just as the sky is higher than the earth,
    so my deeds are superior to your deeds
    and my plans superior to your plans.

Isaiah 55:8-9

Just outside Gainesville, Texas, is a rest stop. I know because I, Tommy Woodard...road warrior, ran out of gas about a mile south of that rest stop on December 14, 1991. I was driving my soon-to-be wife and all my worldly possessions to what would be our new home. And it was late! Like so late it was actually early. My fiancée, now wife, Angie, was asleep in the passenger seat. She suffers from what I call "motion induced narcolepsy." In other words, she falls asleep every time she's in the car!

About 20 miles earlier, the "low fuel" light came on the dashboard. I passed at least 15 gas stations, thinking, *I'll stop at the next one. I'm making good time. I don't want to wake up Angie.* The truth was, I just didn't want to stop and deal with the situation. So...just around midnight I ran out of gas.

Bear in mind this was before the days of cell phones. (Well, cell phones *existed*, but they were the size of bricks, and only rich people had them. And Zach from *Saved by the Bell*.) Which means...I was *stuck*.

After debating my options, I decided to push—that's right, push—the car to the next gas station. I couldn't leave it there on the side of the road; it had all my worldly possessions in it. And I couldn't convince Angie to walk to a gas station and bring me back a few gallons!

OUR SOULS, HEARTS, AND MINDS SEEM TO SHOW US WHEN A "CHECK ENGINE LIGHT" APPEARS IN OUR LIVES. YOU'VE FELT IT, HAVEN'T YOU?

So with my bride-to-be in the driver's seat, I began pushing the car. For the first mile I sang praise songs to God. During the second and third miles I prayed for his strength to make it through the journey. About mile four, I began asking God what I had done that was so wrong that I deserved this kind of punishment.

At mile six, I looked over to the right of the highway and saw giant dogs just beyond a barbed wire fence. I shouted to Angie, "Be careful, there are giant dogs over there!" She replied, "Those are horses, babe...*horses*."

Finally at mile eight I came upon a gas station. I pushed the car up the ramp, filled it up, and went in to pay. The man at the counter looked at me and said, "You run outta gas?" I said, "Yes." However I was thinking, *Nope...I just wanted to get some exercise at 2 a.m. so I decided to push the car for miles on end, you moron!* Since that day, I always fill up the gas tank the minute that light comes on the dash!

You ever done that? Maybe it wasn't the low-fuel light on your dashboard; maybe it was the check engine light. Maybe you've noticed the light just stay on and on and on. Every time you get in the car—"bloop"—there it is. It just stares at you saying, "There's a problem" or at the very least, "Hey, you may want to go in for a tune-up." Instead, you deny it's even there. You even get used to the big glaring orange light and think, *The car seems to be driving fine. I don't have time right now to bring it in to the shop. Besides, they're going to have me pay for a ton of things I really can't afford.*

It's the same inside each of us. Our souls, hearts, and minds seem to show us when a "check engine light" appears in our lives. You've felt it, haven't you? That prompt in your spirit when a relationship isn't quite right. A casual habit that has become something more; something that possesses all your thoughts, all your time, all your money. That lie you keep telling yourself that things aren't really out of hand, and you can stop any time you want. The "check engine" light in your life is glaring, even blaring: "STOP!" But you keep going.

You don't have time, don't have the resources, and if you're really honest, you don't even want to look at the stuff that tends to activate that light.

Let's face it: We do stuff that we really don't want to do. Paul even says it in Romans 7:15: "For I don't understand what I am doing. For I do not do what I want—instead, I do what I hate." So, why do we do it? Because there's a "payoff." As much as we may say we want to quit, stop, or put to death these parts of our lives, there's a part that likes it.

It soothes our soul for an instant—whether it's eating in front of the TV, yelling at those you love, or hanging out with friends you know you shouldn't...you feel control. You're never alone with your thoughts...because the silence and the thought of being alone terrify you. The list of ways that we ignore the check engine light goes on and on, and instead we keep living out the "insanity."

It has been said that insanity is doing the same thing over and over again and expecting different results. Have you ever cried out to someone, "This is insane!?" You were fed up, you'd had enough, and you didn't want this to continue. We throw around the "insanity" term a bit flippantly. We'll talk about traffic being insane or the long line at the grocery store. But it's more about our comfort being disrupted. We hardly ever invoke "insanity" when it comes to the hurt and baggage we tend to carry into our relationships.

This is the point in the book and the chapter of your own life where you get to say, "THIS IS INSANE!"

It's the moment you realize you aren't in control—when you admit that the lifestyle you've been living doesn't work, and it's not really "living."

This is a tough moment for many of us. For some, control comes in a passive-aggressive way; we seem to not care about change or what other people do, but we drop little hints or do things to get our way. For others, we're control freaks. Our worlds for such a long time have been total chaos, and we therefore conclude that we need to control and fast-forward the tape of our lives and the people we love. We don't mean to, but remember: There's a payoff.

So it's time to stop the insanity. It's time to refine the bad habits and ways of communicating that really don't work anymore.

As the stone comes off the sculpture, the artist starts to pick up different tools. Maybe it's the little crease in a stone that needs to be sanded, or a small chisel to help remove a particularly stubborn chunk of stone. Whatever it is, the artist sees it. The artist knows it doesn't belong there. And yet the sculpture holds on to it. That's when the artist lovingly molds the sculpture into the form that he saw in his mind. It takes the deft hands of the sculptor to work the form into something that pleases the eye. As the artist moves and works the stone, he takes care not to strike too hard—rather he aims for just the right spot.

The artist must be in complete control to accomplish his planned sculpture. *Control* is defined as "the power to influence or direct people's behavior or the course of events."

Have you ever found yourself alone on a Saturday night watching one of those police reality shows? The TV screen displays the inside of the squad car, and the cops are chasing down a perp who needs to be brought to justice. The fascinating part of the "cop cam" is watching the way suspects just keep trying to outrun the police: jumping over fences, running through yards, going in different directions until that one moment. That moment where the suspect has nowhere left to run.

When you're sitting there with your bowl of ice cream totally immersed in this piece of tabloid TV, what usually happens? The suspect looks left and then right and then realizes there's no escape. Then they raise their hands in the air. Sometimes they lay facedown and clasp their hands behind their heads. They surrender. They can't control the situation any longer and they stop running.

We, too, must stop running and surrender.

GOD'S CHISEL

Surrender to the fact that God's ways aren't our ways.

Surrender to the fact that God paid the biggest debt when he sent his son.

Surrender to the fact that we can't do it by ourselves.

Surrender to the fact that we can't stop the insanity.

If so, then it's time to choose the chisel.

You don't have to surrender to authorities and be imprisoned. You can choose to surrender your life and will to the Creator of the Universe. You can say "yes" to God and what he did for you. While we are on this earth, we get the chance to refine how we're going to live out this life. God gives us the chance to change.

I remember my moment of surrender: I will never forget it. I don't know how you handle problems but for me...I'm a control freak. I tell people this – "I, Eddie James, am a recovering control freak. My childhood was chaos, I have lived a life of looking ahead, trying to glimpse every possible angle, so that I could determine what the best outcome would be. If I was wrong on the outcome, I'd let anger take over rather than God. If I was correct, I would give myself a pat on the back and give a little glory to God. However you look at it – I was messed up. If the mayor of crazy town had called and asked for the keys to his city, I wouldn't have let them go."

It was nuts—insane—and this was my "normalcy." I remember my wife, Stephanie, had already had two miscarriages and the doctors told us that getting pregnant may be impossible. I remember not having two nickels to rub together and a mountain of debt. I remember wanting "The Skit Guys" to fill my ego more than I wanted God to fill my heart. I remember I couldn't quite figure out how to have relationships without controlling what others should say or experience. I remember thinking, *I can't do this anymore.* And finally, I surrendered. I surrendered to the notion of maybe never having kids. I surrendered the idea that "The Skit Guys" would just be a weekend gig here and there. I surrendered to tithe and not worrying about money. I surrendered to God and invited him to chisel areas of my life that I had been holding on to and controlling. When I surrendered—the chiseling began. And you know what? The joy began...trust me...It can happen for you too.

Take a minute and write down the ways you need to surrender to God.

If you need to use "code words" so that only you and God know what these things are, great. Let's just get them on paper so you can see the truth and what needs to be refined and defined from here on out. It's basically your "I choose the chisel..." list.

I surrender...

1.

2.

3.

4.

Let's go a little deeper. There are probably a few things you are doing that even you can admit, "It's insane." They didn't quite make your "I choose the chisel" list because you still like doing them, or you just have no idea how you can get out of the situation.

Write those down, too. *Come on, you can do it.* These are the habits and actions that you really need God to chisel away—and when he does, you will see great change in your life. It's when God gets much closer to transforming you into his image, his workmanship.

Congratulations! You've just undergone some of the hardest work of your life. They say (okay, I admit I don't really know who "they" is) "awareness is half the battle." What you have done by making these lists is become more aware of the stuff that doesn't "work" anymore. The ways you need to let go of control and allow Christ to intervene on your behalf.

So far in this process:

1. You've taken a hard look in the mirror, and you've made a picture in your heart, soul, and mind of the life you'd like to live with God in control. God is chiseling you in ways that you've never dreamed possible.
2. You've gone even deeper to acknowledge the habits and hurts that seem to have weighed you down all these years. You've chosen to surrender to God and his eternal plan.

This is great stuff. Just like the "God's Chisel" skit, we've only just begun. (By the way, that was a great song by the Carpenters. Not as good as "Muskrat Love" by Captain & Tennille, but it's still a fine love song.) You may need to let this settle down in your soul before moving on. You may want to find a trusted friend or a pastor or someone at church who you can talk to...just to get some things out in the open.

This also may be a perfect time to allow God's chiseling to rough out and refine those areas God has wanted to chip away for quite some time. Don't worry; we (and this book) will be right here waiting for you when you come back.

CHISEL Q'S:

1. Look at Proverbs 3:3. If possible look it up in several different translations. You can find a bunch online or you can go old-school and pull a bunch of different Bibles out of the church basement. Now read Proverbs 3:3. Notice how different translations may use different words for the two important ones. Why do you think this is?

2. Imagine you are carving these words into a flat piece of clay or writing them with your toes in the sand on the beach. Now imagine that the clay has hardened or the sand has become rock. Are you still carving? Imagine God trying to carve these words into your heart. What material is he working with? In general how do you receive advice? For you, personally, is receiving advice like:

☐ A sponge in the rain
☐ A dog getting his belly rubbed
☐ A candle being lit
☐ A brick wall being hit by a glass bottle
☐ A phone receiving a voicemail

What do you think the writer of Proverbs is trying to say?

OPTIONAL:

Take a sheet of paper and write down twenty things that are stressing you out right now. Cut the paper into strips (one strip per stress), fold these strips up, and drop them in a brown lunch bag. Staple it closed. Write down the date thirty days from now on the lunch bag. Now leave the bag alone. Imagine you are giving these things to God. Check it in 30 days. What do you notice?

3. Remember the movie The *Shawshank Redemption*? Turns out ol' Andy was taking the wall of his cell out into the yard a pocket full at a time. How well do you see the big picture? What happens when we look at the wall and see only an obstacle?

4. Imagine your pain, your stress, your guilt...these are stones. Your pockets are full. Now let's go swimming. You know people, you could name them, but don't name them here: Who would drown rather than give up their stones? If you fell out of the boat which stone would you give up first? Yes, we know the BIG one but which one is that to you? What do you suppose makes a person hold on to their pain or fear?

5. Some people have a problem with the word "surrender." It has many negative connotations, so "surrendering" to God is difficult. Use a thesaurus and choose a new word or come up with one on your own. Remember, it still has to mean the same thing. It can't be a word that allows you to hold something back.

CHISEL STORY

I was chiseled when I was 11 years old. Well, it started then. Now I'm 13. When God chiseled me, it was difficult. I had a lot of anger and insecurity in my life. I'm asking God to chisel all of the things that are holding me back from telling people about Him, or even acting like Him.

Katelyn

When God chiseled me, my eyes were opened to understand that no amount of "good-works" was ever going to make me "good enough." Not being "good enough" was not an acceptable way to live and I wanted to refuse to do it. But God said, "no." He chiseled away at my heart and soul until I was humbled enough to be able to understand. You see, I was never going to be the perfect wife or the perfect mother. I could never have been the perfect daughter. God's love/chiseling taught me that this was okay...acceptable. God was willing to meet me right where I was. I was "good enough" for his love. I was "good enough" for his plan. He was proud of me and he did love me, and that would never change. God chisels me yet today. He humbles me from time to time so that I always hear his still, small voice reassuring me that I am and always will be "good enough."

Cynthia

PRAYER:

Close your eyes and imagine your hands out in front of you. You are holding out something. Something dark. Kind of squishy. It smells bad too. You know what it is. You don't have to tell anyone. God already knows.

God, take this. I don't need it anymore. I thought I did but I don't. It was hard to get it out and honestly it's hard to give it up. It's mine. I made it. I had to scrape the edges of my soul to get it all. Take it from me, God. Take it and burn it or do whatever you do with it. Please don't let me feel empty now, God. Please fill that space. Fill the space with your love. Let your love flow into me like water on a hot sidewalk. Fill the cracks. Cool me down. I will be strong. I will be what you called me to be. Amen.

CHAPTER 3

I KNOW WHO'S INSIDE THERE

Wow, that was some hard work. And even though you've admitted the sin and the habits, this is where the hard part begins...and unfortunately where most people give up.

Right now, as you're taking inventory of your life, you're probably realizing that you may have some stunted growth. We're not talking physically, but spiritually or emotionally.

IT'S TIME TO REALLY DIVE DEEP INTO THE GRACE THAT GOD OFFERS EACH OF US.

As hard as that might be to admit, it's even harder to say that it's time to...*grow up*. We know, we know—we sound like your mom right after you broke wind in public and started laughing uncontrollably. But no more excuses, no more stopping and starting—it's time to really dive deep into the grace that God offers each of us. The grace that can give us the ability to change and grow and be more alive in him. (And don't worry, we still laugh at potty humor, and we're all grown up...kinda!)

Okay, let's get started. It's one thing to notice all the negative stuff and write it all down, but it's quite another to roll up our sleeves and get to the self-work that needs doing. This is hard work. But it's worth it.

There is a great illustration on this subject in the movie *A League of Their Own*. The Rockford Peaches baseball coach Jimmy Dugan (Tom Hanks) gives Dottie Hinson (Geena Davis) a straightforward lecture when she sneaks away from the team after her husband returns from World War II. Her husband finds her on the road and wants her to come back home and be a wife and give up her "dream" of playing baseball:

Jimmy: Taking a little day trip?

Dottie: No, Bob and I are driving home. To Oregon.

Jimmy: [long pause] You know, I really thought you were a ballplayer.

Dottie: Well, you were wrong.

Jimmy: Was I?

Dottie: Yeah. It is only a game, Jimmy. It's only a game, and, and, I don't need this. I have Bob; I don't need this. At all.

Jimmy: I, I gave away five years at the end of my career to drink. Five years. And now there isn't anything I wouldn't give to get back any one day of it.

Dottie: Well, we're different.

Jimmy: (*expletive*) Dottie, if you want to go back to Oregon and make a hundred babies, great. I'm in no position to tell anyone how to live. But sneaking out like this, quitting, you'll regret it for the rest of your life. Baseball is what gets inside you. It's what lights you up; you can't deny that.

Dottie: It just got too hard.

Jimmy: It's supposed to be hard. If it wasn't hard, everyone would do it. The "hard"...is what makes it great.

So you're faced with an ultimatum: Stay where you are spiritually...or allow God to work in and through you to be everything he planned you to be. Ultimatums demand a decision, and may call for hard work.

My first year in college I decided I wanted to be an accountant. My father said, "Tommy, go get a communications degree." But I didn't listen. I was going to be an accountant! (I know it's dumb...I can't even count! Just go with me here.) I took Accounting 101 at 10 a.m. every Monday and Wednesday. Since it was my first semester, I went to every class. (That would change drastically as the years went on.) I knew I wasn't doing well because I didn't really understand anything that was being taught. So around finals time, I went to my professor and asked a simple question: "Can I pass your class?"

She looked at my grades, paused, and without looking up replied, "No."

I stood there for a moment and then began to exit her office feeling like Charlie Brown right after he tries to kick the football Lucy was holding on the grass. As I got to the door, she said, "By the way, what is your major?" I replied, "Accounting." There was a long silent pause as we both stared at each other. She was thinking about how dumb it was for me to be an accounting major; I was thinking about where I would go for lunch.

She broke the silence. "I'll tell you what. IF you pass the final AND promise to change your major, I will GIVE YOU a passing grade in my class." I said, "You've got a deal!" and went to Dairy Queen to celebrate.

My professor had given me an ultimatum, so what did I do?

I KNOW WHO'S INSIDE THERE

Over the next few days, I studied hard for the Accounting 101 final. My friends helped me and quizzed me. It was a lot of work, but it was worth it. In the end, I got a 73 percent on the final and to this day I have a "D" in Accounting 101 on my official transcript.

Oh yeah, and I changed my major to oral communications... much better for a Skit Guy!

Think about it: We've all been faced with ultimatums.

- Try out for the basketball team or just watch from the sidelines.
- Work hard for the promotion or just get the job done.
- Start over on your artwork or tell yourself you can't do it.
- Work on your marriage or give up.
- Study hard to get a passing grade in accounting or... oh wait, that was just me.

You could pursue that dream or keep things status quo. When was the last time you went for it? How many people have you seen go after those dreams? In my life, not many. Dreams can seem intangible and unattainable. They bring way too much risk, and we resort to fast-forwarding the tapes of our worlds to see the humiliation that we would suffer. Whether that anticipated humiliation might come from friends or family or even the "critics" of our world, if we tried and failed...we'd never live it down.

But what if? What if you took the road less traveled? What if you did the hard work, and you discovered just as Tom Hanks' character describes, "what makes it great"?

So far you've looked hard at your life. And that's good. That's the first thing that needs to happen when you choose the chisel. BUT, that's just the beginning. Admitting and recognizing are amazing steps toward growth. But that's all they are: amazing steps. YOU have to start stepping toward your new life. Toward some painful chisel-type chapters in your world.

And make no mistake...it will be:

Hard.
Tough.
Not fun.
Uncomfortable.
Rocky.
Lonely.
Unsettling.
Exhilarating.

Just keep in mind Jimmy Dugan's words: "THE HARD IS

WHAT MAKES IT GREAT." The chiseling our God wants to do with you is what makes it GREAT!

Are you ready for this type of chiseling?

Are you ready to do the hard work?

If we skip a meal, there's no part of us that says in wild despair, "What's the use? I missed a meal. I might as well not eat the rest of the day! It's over!"

Yet we do that when it comes to the spiritual conditions of our hearts. We make the unwise choice that has a ripple effect and we just "give up."

"What's the use?!" we cry out to God.

We cry out to ourselves: "I've messed up."

There's no hope, we argue. There's no way God could use us after the decisions we've made and the hurt we've caused others. We argue that God can only be "tolerating" us at this point.

WHEN IT COMES TO OUR RELATIONSHIP WITH GOD...WHY DO WE THINK WE WERE EVER DOING THE "HOLDING UP"?

But that's not the character of God. In Jeremiah 31, the Lord says, "I have loved you with an everlasting love. That is why I have continued to be faithful to you."

Do you get that? God is faithful to love us no matter what!

In "God's Chisel," we see a couple of statements:

YOU: I was thinking...

GOD: Your thoughts are not my thoughts.

YOU: Yeah, but if there was another way...

GOD: Your ways are not my ways. (Isaiah 55:8)

YOU: It doesn't matter. (halfway defeated)

GOD: What doesn't?

YOU: Never mind. You wouldn't understand.

GOD: I, God of all the universe, wouldn't understand something one of my children has to say to me? Try me.

YOU: (with tears in your eyes as you think about your hurts and scarred past) I've let you down so many times, God.

GOD: You were never holding me up. I hold you up with my victorious, righteous, right hand. (Isaiah 41:10)

When it comes to our relationship with God...Why do we think we were ever doing the "holding up"? It's crazy, isn't it? But we all do it. At some point we all figure we were the ones holding it all together. Where did we ever get the tables turned thinking it was all on our shoulders to be perfect? To do it all?

It's hard work to stop and surrender. So do a 180 and get to the hard work. It's hard to accept the fact we don't have to hold up God in our relationship with him through our actions and words. What a mess things would be if God depended on us to hold him up!

He.
Holds.
Us.
Up.

That should give you freedom. That should allow some rays of grace (Remember? God's undeserved favor for you...) to enter those remote, dark spots of your hurting soul. That should bring some relief.

It reminds me of a time when I was a ring bearer in a wedding. Can't you picture little bucktoothed Tommy in a 1970's white tuxedo! So I was a ring bearer and my older sister was a candle lighter. Picture this: The church sanctuary is filled with people. The pipe organ is playing, and my sister starts walking down the aisle with one of those huge, old ornate brass church candle lighter things. About halfway down the aisle, the wick on the candle lighter extinguishes. She was walking too fast. She panics and has no idea what to do. She stops for a moment. Then decides she will just go through the motions and pretend to light the candles. While this is not a good idea, it's the only idea she has. Tears begin to stream down her face as she heads down the aisle again. The voices in her head shout at her, "You look stupid! Everyone knows you screwed up! You are a failure!" But she keeps walking down the aisle.

Then, just as she's about six rows back from the candelabras, a lone figure stands up. It's our dad. He reaches in his pocket, pulls out a lighter, strikes it, and with a smile on his face says to her, "Flick of the Bic?" Her tears are now graced with a smile and slight chuckle. Dad relit the candle lighter, and my sister went on to accomplish her purpose in the wedding ceremony.

Okay…so now we know a few more things:

1. It's going to be hard to change.
2. We don't carry the weight of the world on our shoulders.
3. God loves us like crazy. In a totally crazy, grace-filled way. More than we could ever imagine sort of way.

So…what's keeping you from making those changes? More

importantly—what's holding you back from using your gifts and talents for God? What's stopping you from following those crazy dreams God has put in your heart and ultimately making HIM famous? (Remember—it's not about us.)

When we first started traveling as the Skit Guys, one of us lived in California and the other one lived in Texas. People would fly us in to do their events. During that first year or two, it seemed like something would go wrong with every event we would try to do. A flight would get canceled. Weather would delay us. Someone would die on the plane we were on, and they would make an emergency landing. (No lie—that actually happened!) It seemed as though this ministry wasn't going to make it. It felt like this dream of using our gifts and talents for God's kingdom would always be nothing more than a dream. But we decided that nothing was going to stop us from being and doing everything God had planned for us! NOTHING!

Look at these lines from "God's Chisel":

> YOU: Go ahead and chisel away. But be prepared for what you're going to find in there. Because I know who's inside there. I get up every morning and look in the mirror. Inside is the scared, stupid little kid. I dress like an adult and I try to act like an adult, but I can't. I can't be who everyone wants me to be. I can't even be who I want to be, much less who you created me to be. So go ahead, chisel away, but just be prepared for what you are going to find.

Inside each of us there's a little boy or a little girl that has either been nurtured emotionally and spiritually to grow up if you had a great environment and family—and maybe you also got to learn about the precepts of faith in God. But for a lot of us, we have this stunted growth—this little boy or little girl still trying to prove himself or herself to others and even to God.

In my office pinned to a bulletin board is a short email from my dad. It's been there for years. The primary purpose of the email was to let me know that our family was having dinner in a couple of days. But that's not why it hangs in my office. It was the P.S. part of the email that simply says these words, "Tommy, I am so proud of you." My dad had no idea how important it was for me to hear that from him. He was just sharing his feelings with me. But it was so important that years later I look at it almost daily to remember that I'm more than okay with my dad...I am a source of his pride.

Maybe we're still—even as our bodies get older—chasing after that stamp of approval we never got.

Maybe we yearn to hear someone say, "I'm so proud of you son" or "Daughter, you are beautiful on the inside and out."

YOU ARE BEAUTIFUL INSIDE AND OUT.

I KNOW WHO'S INSIDE THERE

The phrases relating to your own needed stamp of approval can vary, but regardless your life suffered from a "chasing after" love for a really long time.

And maybe the road of your life is filled with unforgettable stamps of approval that seemed right at the time but led down a road that was...empty.

Remember that definition of *insanity*? You and I, we've traveled down these roads time and time again until we just feel defeated. And then, at the end, we throw up our hands and cry to our Creator, "Chisel away...but be ready for what you're going to find in there. 'Cause I already know..."

We've listened to so many voices for far too long...and they've said, "You are junk."

You are...
No good.
Washed up.
Stupid.
Trouble.
Useless.
A disappointment.
Not what we wanted.

Ultimately, we've walked along in this world as orphans.

Look what Psalm 86:15 says: "But you, O Lord, are a

compassionate and merciful God. You are patient and demonstrate great loyal love and faithfulness."

Think about what that verse says...You are loved by the Father, the Creator of this Universe. He is compassionate, merciful, patient, loyal, and faithful to you. When you do the work and then realize that God already knows what he's going to find...you can start to dream. Because he wants to help you grow up so you can use your talents and gifts to make him famous.

"God can do anything, you know—far more than you could ever imagine or guess or request in your wildest dreams! He does it not by pushing us around but by working within us, his Spirit deeply and gently within us."—Ephesians 3:20 (*The Message*)

I KNOW WHO'S INSIDE THERE

Here's some work:

Take some time and write and dream and imagine what you could do with your life to make God smile.

Go somewhere that allows you to dream and imagine.

We will wait. Take your time.

MY DREAM...

CHISEL Q'S:

1. Remember that list we showed you on page 72?

   Hard
   Tough
   Not fun
   Uncomfortable.
   Rocky
   Lonely
   Unsettling
   Exhilarating

   Now...think about *Sesame Street*? The PBS show used to play a game called "One of these Things Is Not Like the Other." Can you spot the word that doesn't seem to fit in this list?

2. Imagine your life is one of those lines you see on the EKG monitor. Draw that in the space below. Choose ten events (bad and good) from your life in the last year or two. Place those in points on your lifeline. What was the highest point? What was your lowest? What happens if life has no highs or lows?

3. Read Psalm 86. It's filled with highs and lows. What it doesn't do is question God. The lyrics we find in the Psalms are euphoric and tragic but in all instances they recognize God is in charge.

   Why is it so easy to think God is picking on us during bad times?

4. Sometimes we put on a different person like we put on different clothes. Is there a difference between the "you" outside your home and the "you" at home? What about the "you" that goes to church?

5. Have you ever pretended to like a particular band, movie, podcast, or some other media simply so you can be part of the conversation? How often do you see that in other people?

6. Who do you know that is completely themselves? How old are they? Why does it seem like some older people are able to be themselves and not care what other people think?

7. God is trying to chisel these bits away from you. These bits are the fake or pretend you...the you trying to be someone else. Sometimes the little ones hurt the most...the ones closest to the skin. Why are you so attached to these bits? Why are we often afraid to be vulnerable? In what way are these extra chunks of rock around us protecting us from the outside world?

CHISEL STORY

The first time I watched "God's Chisel" I...was ministered, humbled, and compelled to bring it to my church, and we did it in Spanish and I was glad I was able to share the blessing I received from God through your script to my brothers and sisters.

When God chiseled me...I felt relieved, lightweight, but I know more needs to be done.

I am asking God to chisel...everything and anything he sees in me that is not from him, that is preventing a closer relationship to him.

Miguel

> The first time I saw "God's Chisel" I was scared but I knew that he had a plan for my life. When God chiseled me he took away my addiction to alcohol. I was chiseled 7 years ago.
>
> Deana

PRAYER:

Creator God, take your time with us. Be precise. We hang on so tightly to things we don't need. We would dip ourselves in plaster if we thought it would protect us from the kind of hurt we feel. Free us, God. We will steady ourselves for the pain that comes from letting things go. Show us we don't need to collect those stones and try to glue them back in place. Give us the euphoria that comes with being free of the rock that has been trapping us all along. Amen.

You may at times just need to put this book down and work out these components in your life. That's how the book was designed. You do some work and come back to the book. But whatever you do, don't forget about us. We still have a few more chapters to go!

CHAPTER 4
YOU ARE NOT JUNK

You have listened to so many voices besides mine for far too long and you have really bought into the lie. You think you're junk, don't you? When you've laid your head down at night after "doing the dance, to get the hug" from so many people, you think you are junk.

I praise you because I am fearfully and wonderfully made; your works are wonderful, I know that full well.—Psalm 139:14 (NIV)

"You've made this day a special day, by just your being you. There's no person in the whole world like you, and I like you, just the way you are."—Mr. Rogers

WE HURT, THEREFORE WE COLLECT...
JUNK IN OUR LIVES.

Have you ever watched the T.V. show *Hoarders*? (If not go search for it online now. If you can't find your computer... you may be a hoarder!) Sometimes I sit there slightly amused and mildly nauseated by the amount of junk one person can collect. And then...I see the destruction of the junk. You see how it has affected others, and then we see them doing the hard work to get rid of the junk. In one episode, they actually found a dead body in someone's house under all the junk! Can you imagine?

I find it interesting that during the "work" part of the show, a lot of them want to quit. They don't really want to do the work.

It's at that part of the show that I can relate. I've quit before. I've given up doing the hard work. "Eddie, don't give up. You've come too far." That's what I heard John Baker, my sponsor say to me. I did every step he told me. I answered all the questions as far as, "Who have I hurt? Who do I need to go make amends to?" But the question that was making me give up was, "What part – with this person – of your past are you responsible for?" I sat there coming up with all kinds of "common" answers but even as they came out of my mouth they weren't right: "Well, if I had been good enough?." "If I tried to do more to keep them from being angry at me." "If I had tried harder then maybe..." But with every answer, every brain cell bursting to just say the right thing — I was done. The work was officially too hard and I didn't want to go there. He asked again, "Eddie — what did you do to deserve this in this relationship?" I sat there like a little boy. I was always good with words and now I had nothing. There had to be an answer to make everything be alright but there wasn't. And then — it hit me... with tears in my eyes it came tumbling out of my mouth — "Nothing! — I did *nothing* to deserve the type of treatment in this relationship." I had been running so fast to avoid the real issues. I had been working so hard to do the dance to just get the hug for far too long. Then I realized, people cannot give what they do not have. That blinding light was the grace that God gave me that day... it was like a big ol' blanket of his crazy love. It was truly my *Good Will Hunting* moment except I wasn't a math wiz and my sponsor/counselor didn't get his fame from starting out as *Mork from Ork*. If I hadn't carried out the work, I would have never known the most precious word to me at that time and still today: nothing.

Have you ever felt that way? Have you found yourself wanting to just quit and settle back into your normal rhythm and routine? You know, living your life like nothing has changed... like you've been doing for the past month? Several years? Decade?

The work, the change, the veil being lifted from the confusion we have lived makes us want to run away. We want to blame and accuse others for our "junk."

Think about it though...do you really believe these people woke up one day and said, "I really think it would be beneficial to me and others if I started collecting my Taco Bueno trash. And those broken light bulbs over there, I need to keep them. And those Snuggies...that I found in my neighbor's trash...I need those. And I need to keep all of it. It might come in handy one day."

When you stop to think about it...they really didn't want this for themselves. They didn't set out to be a collector of everything "unholy." Interestingly enough, there's always a part in the show that allows us to peek at what made this Hoarder the way he or she is...hurt. There was a past pain that influenced that person to stop living and start collecting junk.

I find myself doing that, too...in ways. At points in of our lives we allow our hurt to just stop us.

We may not collect Ore Ida French Fry plastic containers, but we do collect.

Anger
Bitterness
Regret

YOU ARE NOT JUNK

Jealousy
Addictions

On and on. Just to numb the pain.

We hurt, therefore we collect…junk in our lives.

We become hoarders of a different sort. We don't want the cameras on us for the world to see. We don't want peering eyes to observe the damage we've done to ourselves and others. We collect the junk—therefore we think we must be junk, too.

"NOT TRUE!" says the one true God who pours out his love upon us. Look at this fascinating piece of Scripture concerning YOU:

No, in all these things we have complete victory through him who loved us! For I am convinced that neither death, nor life, nor angels, nor heavenly rulers, nor things that are present, nor things to come, nor powers, nor height, nor depth, nor anything else in creation will be able to separate us from the love of God in Christ Jesus our Lord.—Romans 8:37–39 (NET)

We discussed this love in chapter 1 by way of Psalm 139. We've talked about living out your dream in chapter 3. And now for a extra little tug to help us get out of the junk. To not retreat to the old ways. To not hoard the old life and avoid walking in the new…

GOD'S CHISEL

What does it look like to live in a new home?

What does it look like to respond instead of react to the world and chaos around you?

What does it feel like to allow God to keep chiseling and you simply living in the beautiful fact that...

You.
Are.
Not.
Junk.

In the 1970s some Christians wore buttons with a bunch of letters strewn together like this:

PBPWMGINTWMY.

What in the world?

When I was a little kid...and yes, I did have hair...I remember asking this question to a button-wearer once after she'd displayed it several days in a row. I was only about five years old, but I'll never forget what she told me:

"Please Be Patient With Me. God Is Not Through With Me Yet."

I think that basically sums it all up. I mean, really...isn't that what choosing the chisel is all about? We're saying to the world, "I don't have this all together. I'm choosing not to hoard past failures. I'm choosing not to live in the lie. I need your patience as I try to be patient with myself. Philippians 1:6 comforts me with the fact that God is doing a great work in me, and I know he is faithful to complete it."

At the ripe old age of five, I had no idea what that button phrase meant. I had no clue what a teenager could mean by that…let alone an adult.

I do now.

I get it.

It's the only way that I know how to live most days.

We never cross the finish line on this earth. We get to run the race and look toward heaven. All the accolades, all the significance we can achieve on this earth is really "garbage" compared to hearing God say:

"Well done, good and faithful servant."–Matthew 25:21 (NIV)

Would the God of the universe give us a book that states what our end looks like if we were junk?

If we are junk, what does that say about God, since we're created in his image?

I struggle from time to time thinking I'm junk. Thinking about my past failures. Thinking they define my life. But I have to remind myself to be patient— to say to myself, "Ed, God isn't through chiseling you." I haven't reached the finish line. Paul reminds me to leave the past behind and run the race set before me. To love God because God first loved me. Loved you. Loved us.

IF WE ARE JUNK, WHAT DOES THAT SAY ABOUT GOD, SINCE WE'RE CREATED IN HIS IMAGE?

God gave his one and only son for you...think about that...and then think about what you're still holding on to? What junk do you still hoard?

Also, have you noticed on *Hoarders*, as the crew of cleaners throws stuff away, the hoarder is right there at times saying, "No! Not that. I'm keeping that!"

The great thing about our spiritual situation is that God does the work. He allows us to be a part of it, but mostly he calls us to rest in him and allow him to work through us.

My family moved across town the summer just before I entered the 4th grade. We worked all day moving all our furniture and the stuff we had collected over the years. Near the end of the day we had one thing left to move...a piano.

So my dad, his friend, and I all pulled, pushed, and lifted that big old piano out of our old house, into a box truck, and into our new house. When we were all done, I shared a big glass jar of Gatorade with my dad. I was so proud of the work I had done. I remember saying to him, "I can't believe I just moved a piano!" My dad just smiled and said, "You sure did Tommy."

Looking back on that experience, I realize the truth of that day is that I didn't do the work. More than likely, I was *in the way* more than I helped. The truth is that Dad did all the work. He just wanted me to be part of the experience because he knew I would experience the satisfaction of accomplishing something after it was over.

In your life, you will not do the work alone that may need doing. God has a plan to work in you and through you to accomplish his plan for your life. But he also has other people, maybe even people you don't know yet, who are willing to help you through this process. That may seem crazy or even scary because no one wants to expose his or her deep secrets to anyone else. But that's one of the reasons God created the church—to help us through the difficulties of struggling with our old lives.

If you're going to enjoy living in that life you wrote about in chapter 1, then you'll have to let go of some old habits, hurts, and hang-ups as you trust God to move things out. Not many of us are good at letting go, though. In fact, most of our difficulties can be traced back to those old things we've been holding on to.

We have become spiritual hoarders.

In the Gospels, you see Jesus encounter spiritual hoarders known as Pharisees. They were holding on to their old way of life. It didn't matter that it wasn't working for them; they just couldn't let go of it. While they looked fine on the outside, they were dead on the inside and unwilling to look at a new way of life in Christ. But we don't have to hold on to our old ways. The work Jesus did on the cross makes you new and sets you free from your old life.

While we've been made alive in Christ and set free, we can still hold on to unhealthy aspects of our old lives. Like a hoarder, we may possess things we don't want to let go of. And maybe they're filled with secret sins. We know these secret sins are unhealthy for us, but we somehow need them...maybe even enjoy them.

What am I saying? We *LOVE* them.

We love them and don't want to let them go.

The downside is that our enjoyment feels good only for a moment. Sin seems to heal the wound for a little while, but ultimately it leads to us hearing that voice that we've heard over and over: "You are junk. Look at you. You are pathetic.

Did you really think you were going to change and live this new life? That's for others, not you."

That lie can't win.

No, that lie won't win.

Wait…not even that…that lie already lost.

Thankfully Jesus has conquered that lie.

So, let's be patient with one another as we look at the junk we collect.

We know what you're saying: "If I turn that page and have to grab a pen, I'm going to throw this book across the room." Well, go ahead and throw it across the room. (If you're a hoarder don't do that…You'll never see this book again.)

Well, go ahead and throw it across the room. Then at some point after you've calmed down, pick it up from the potted plant that now looks like it was mangled by a lizard and…turn the page.

What is the junk you find yourself hoarding?

What are those things in your walk with God that get you saying, "God, I'm giving you 90 percent of my life, but this 10 percent I don't know how to throw away."

Write down the "junk":

JUNK:
1.

2.

3.

4.

5.

6.

7.

Let's state the new obvious.

We don't care where you're at right now. Coffee shop, Grandma's house, in your car listening to this as an audio book, out by the lake (and yeah, lying on your bed...that's cool, too...just trying to be imaginative with our locations).

YOU ARE NOT JUNK

Say this out loud: "I AM NOT JUNK."

Say it again. "I AM NOT JUNK."

Say it like you mean it! "I AM NOT JUNK."

That's right. You are not junk. God doesn't take time to sculpt junk. But it seems every time you want to send yourself a "message" that says...

I'm such a klutz.
I'm so stupid.
I am the worst.
Why would anyone want to be with me?
Who do I think I am?
I blow it every time.

You know the "junk" messages you send yourself. We want you to work on those. When you get "junk" messages in email, you eventually move them to the trash. We'd suggest you start thinking of all these messages as "junk" mail...stuff that will bring you down and won't delight God. Instead of filling your inbox with all those lies and spam, block them and trash them!

We want you to work on letting go of that 10 percent you hold on to so dearly—stuff that really isn't of God. It's junk.

Because we aren't defined by the junk.

CHISEL Q'S:

Just for fun come up with your own cram-the-first-letters-together phrase. This one is our favorite. WWMJBMOHN? (What Would Make Jesus Blow Milk Out of His Nose?) Don't get us started...there's a whole 'nuther book in that question.

1. What would happen if, for just one day, everyone had to wear a T-shirt with one word printed on the front. That one word (okay maybe two) is how that person in their heart of hearts defines themselves.

    • Would you see any words repeated?

    • What would you say to someone who has "last picked" on their shirt?

    • What would Jesus say to "too busy," "loser," "stressed-out"?

    • What would Jesus say to you when he saw your shirt?

2. Would you consider yourself one of those people who had to touch the wet paint in order to believe the sign? Have you ever touched a hot stove or held your hand over a candle? David was one of those people. (David the giant killer, street musician, dancer, voyeur, warrior, adulterer, insomniac, king.)

   Does your life fit you like a pair of comfortable slippers or a pair of pants that are too tight? (Come up with your own analogy if you want to.)

3. Read Psalm 40. If you have multiple translations available to you, read this same Psalm in each of them. Which one speaks to you the most? Why?

   Break the Psalm down this way. Come up with a short phrase for each of the sections of this Psalm.

   verses 1-3   How God lets the world know he is there.

verses 4-5   How God works in your life.

verses 6-8   What have you or what are you willing to give up for God?

verses 9-10   How do you tell others about God?

verses 11-15 How would you like God to intervene in your life right now?

verses 15-17 How would you like God to intervene for others?

PRAYER:

God, we need to breathe. We spend so much time trying to be someone or something else. We spend so much time allowing those who don't even know us to define us. Their opinion means nothing. If someone does not like us for who we are, that should not be our problem. Help us to see ourselves as your creation. Help us to see the world as if everyone was wearing a T-shirt that said, "GOD'S." Help us to understand that we are all miracles. Amen.

YOUR PERSONAL MANIFESTO

What is God calling you to do? What are you created to do?

You are a masterpiece.

We want you to put the book down right now and grab a mirror. We know, we know...it's uncomfortable and awkward, but it's good. Grab a mirror and say these words out loud:

"I am God's Masterpiece."

Okay...we'll wait. Seriously. Just put the book down and do it. Okay...now do it again. Come on, you can do it. Here, we'll do it with you...count of three, okay? *One...two...three...*

AND for the ones that couldn't get up to look in a mirror or just felt like that would be crazy sauce – at some point – find a mirror and just say it. Go for it.

Yes. Yes, you are. You are a masterpiece with hopes and

dreams. You are an original piece of God's handiwork. Not some random piece of extra scrap material in the craftsman's workshop, but a one-of-a-kind original. In this world of billions there is no one like you. From the tips of your fingers and those crevices that we call fingerprints down to the tips of your toes and all the way into those synapses in your brain, no one is quite like you. Sure there might be people who are similar to you...but none are YOU. (Besides, you know only you make that weird chortle when you laugh...no one does that but you.)

You are unique.
You are God created.
You are valuable.
You are precious in his sight.

The whole idea of the "God's Chisel" skit is to try to break through the cluttered and messy messages that this world throws at us. From telling us that we're not smart enough, not pretty enough, fast enough, handsome enough, rich enough, thin enough—almost anything that you can put in front of "enough" is fair game. **But the world is feeding us a lie.**

You are God's beloved, just as you are.

Now, that doesn't mean (as we've been discussing) that God wants you to stay stagnant and stuck. No, he's got great big plans for you. But he won't love you any more or less no matter where you are in your story. You are his beloved, which means you are GREATLY LOVED. That has got to feel good, right? Come on, I see you smiling. Even from behind that big wall you use for hiding. Isn't it great to know the Creator of the Universe loves you and no one – no one – can take that fact away?

Check out this verse from which GOD'S CHISEL was born: Ephesians 2:10,

> *For we are his workmanship, having been created in Christ Jesus for good works that God prepared beforehand so we may do them.*

In the original Greek writing of this verse, the word translated *workmanship* is "poiema"–this is where we get the English word "poem." Another way of looking at this is that you are God's poem–his work of art.

Okay, so you're probably thinking, *This has been a good journey*, as you have explored this book and journaled and worked and cried and done some healing. This chapter should almost feel like a graduation ceremony. Where we call your name and you walk across the platform with your family and friends cheering you on, chanting your name, shaking the scene like a Polaroid instant photo.

Nope. There's still one more thing we want you to do.

Turn the page...

So if you threw this book against the wall and are now picking it up and reading to the last part of this journey, hooray for you! If you need to throw it against the wall once more, we completely understand. In fact, we made these books with throw-against-the-wall fibers so it stands the test of time (and tempers).

CHISEL Q'S:

1. Think about the commercials that you've seen or heard... which commercial tells the biggest lie?

2. In what ways does the world expect you to fit into the mold of what you "should" be?

3. What does the word PURPOSE mean? (Come on now...don't whip out your phone and look it up.) Think about it...come up with several definitions.

4. Take a couple minutes and just let your mind run free...what pops up from your life. Anything you want to write? We'll even get you started. Ready?

Hot fudge, zombie movies, Oreos, Saturday mornings, homework, computer crashes, peas...

Good Things	Bad Things

That verse we asked you to read from Ephesians…read it again.

Now look at 2 Corinthians 5:17.
Now read Romans 8:28.

In some of the oldest written texts we know these three verses all contain similar references to things of God's making. God is creating something in these verses. In Romans God is taking all things…ALL THINGS…and making them work for his purposes.

God does not make messes in your life. Stuff happens. God will take it and make it work with everything else and use it for his purposes.

PRAYER:

God I am who I am. I am stronger. I am valued. I am amazing. I am wonderful. I am unique. I am all these things because of you. I will open my life to you. I will give you everything. My joys and my stresses. You know what to do with them. I will create something in me. I will be a new creation. Amen.

Here's the last thing. We want you to write a manifesto.

Manifesto: a written statement declaring publicly the intentions, motives, or views of the issuer. A call to action.

Let that word sink in for a minute. Even say it a few times fast. (It's kind of hard to do.) This is your *Braveheart* moment. This is you declaring to all the "critics" and all the "naysayers" out there what you are all about and that you don't mind fighting for every inch of character and every part of your God-given talents and gifts in order to make him famous.

This is a big moment. You couldn't have gotten to this point without doing the previous chapters. You have arrived here, but it would be a shame just to leave you here. So let's have a look at the future a little. Let's give yourself a road map to refer to when the "trappings of this world" come along—so you don't fall for them.

The word *manifesto* has taken on some strong connotations over the years. And rightly so…it's a strong word. You're declaring publicly what you want to be about. And whether it's a government doing the declaring or a person, *manifesto* is a loaded word.

But think about it from the perspective of the person who created it. They've sat down and drafted a document to tell other people (remember—it's public, not hidden) what they are about.

I don't know about you, but that scares me. I like a certain amount of flexibility when it comes to life, but with a manifesto, you're basically saying, "This is who I am, this is what I'm about, and this is why I'm doing what I'm doing."

If you follow Christ's teaching...this is where the rubber meets the road. It's one thing to go to church each week. Attend Bible study. Bring donuts on the Sunday you're assigned. It's quite another thing to actually write down a document of your personal call to action.

A few weeks ago in our church the eighth-graders got up in front of everyone and read their manifestos. Sure, they followed a formula, but they were their views about Jesus, God, the Holy Spirit, the Body of Christ, etc. And in them they described how they interacted with each. If you truly believe in Jesus, doesn't that impact how you live each and every day. Shouldn't it?

Of course each of us will mess up and go off our manifesto from time to time...but the fact that you have a goal—a bull's-eye you're focusing on—that will help keep you on track. And when you do mess up, it will point you back in the right direction.

So...how about it? You ready to create your own personal manifesto?

We'll leave some space in the book here, but really...you'll probably want to sit at a computer or grab a pen and paper. Go on...get the pen...now the paper. Okay. Ready? Good.

THINK ABOUT YOUR LIFE

What are the most important things to you?

How do you want others to think about you?

When you leave the room, what do you want other people to say about you?

When your friends remember you, what's the first thing you want popping into their minds?

What are your gifts and talents, and how are you using them?

In what ways is it time to start using your gifts and talents?

What do you want to do with your life?

Fast-forward the tape and think about sitting with your grandchildren...what stories do you want to tell them?

Will those stories be about how you helped people? How you stood up for what was right?

Looking at your life from the other side of the lens sometimes helps to bring clarity.

GET SPECIFIC

Are there statements you could make? Things you want to do? Think in specifics now…not general terms. Such as:

I want to have kids.

I want to visit Uruguay.

I want to own a Gremlin (the car, not the cute furry animal).

I don't want to have kids.

I want to get married.

I don't want to get married.

I want to become a pastor.

I want to become a CEO.

I want to own my own cupcake business.

I want to read through the Bible in a year.

I want to read through the Psalms in a year.

I want to serve the homeless in my community.

I want to serve those imprisoned in my community.

Get specific. And just come up with a long list of things. Don't worry if you think others won't like what you write down…this is your list, and if you write it on paper, you can always burn it when you're done with this whole exercise!

Seriously though, this is for your eyes only if you want.

NOW...CONSOLIDATE

As you look over your list (whether it's one page or 10 pages), think about different categories that you could put each item into. Maybe think about this as taking those individual statements and creating buckets to put them in...you're grouping them together and hopefully they play nice!

Talk to the Future You

What does life look like as far as dreams and goals in the next year?

What does life look like as far as dreams and goals in the next five years?

Ten years?

Take some time and write these out. Sit somewhere over coffee or whatever that favorite place is where you can think. We invest our time in so many useless pursuits, but we never really sit down and write out what our life could look like in the next decade. Proverbs 16:9 says, "A person plans his course, but the LORD directs his steps." While God is in charge of directing our paths, we still have the opportunity and bear the responsibility to plan, make goals, and dream!

You see that? There can be a road map when it comes to living the Christian life and trying to make God famous.

Here are some key areas to get you started thinking about your future:

Personal
Work
Home life (i.e., your family—different than "personal life")
Friends
Dreams

Making God Famous

How can you use where you are, with what you've been given, to start using your gifts and talents to make God famous in your city? Your world? If you're not doing it, why aren't you?

Holding on to the Past

What hurts, habits, or hang-ups are you still holding on to? Write them down. There is power in writing these down and actually looking at them. Circle the one that you're going to work on letting go of and giving to God. Then come back and work through these hurts until you're free. (Make sure these are part of your one-year to 10-year plan regarding the "future you.")

Talk to God

We talked about you being God's poem. Now...write your poem to God. How do you want to live out your life for him? Talk about your love for him, your need for him, your desires while you're on this earth. This is different than "how" you want to make God famous—this is you simply praising him. In the end, this is what we get to do—to walk with Christ and praise his holy name.

Well, you did it! This is where we'd have you walk across the platform and look into your eyes and say, "Job well done."

But we don't get to do that, do we? So, just pat yourself on the back and be gentle on yourself as you navigate these next chapters of your life. Know that in the end, that's exactly what we get to hear as believers and followers of God: "Well done good and faithful servant." (Matthew 25:23) Isn't that amazing? The Creator of the Universe gives us the ultimate stamp of approval at the end of our lives no matter who has or hasn't given us that stamp of approval during our lives. God says, "Good job!"

So let's live like this as we have great days, stumble and fall on other days, experience heartache over seasons, and acknowledge in humility that we get to serve God with our own DNA.

Think about it...Genesis started with God saying "It is good...It is very good." And that's exactly how it will end when He finishes chiseling your life. He'll look at you and say "It is very good!" Let's choose the chisel. Let's help others. Let's be different people.

We would love to hear your story as it's still unfolding. Send it to us at chisel@skitguys.com. We'd also love to see pictures of your cats dressed as famous people through history; if you do that follow us on instagram@skitguys.